BEGINNING PIANO SOLO

HAPPY SONGS • 10 Fun Songs Arranged

T0087035

HAPPY SONGS

ISBN 978-1-5400-9492-6

Visit Hal Leonard Online at
www.halleonard.com

Contact us:
Hal Leonard
7777 West Bluemound Road
Milwaukee, WI 53213
Email: info@halleonard.com

In Europe, contact:
Hal Leonard Europe Limited
42 Wigmore Street
Marylebone, London, W1U 2RN
Email: info@halleonardeurope.com

In Australia, contact:
Hal Leonard Australia Pty. Ltd.
4 Lentara Court
Cheltenham, Victoria, 3192 Australia
Email: info@halleonard.com.au

CONTENTS

AC-CENT-TCHU-ATE THE POSITIVE

from the Motion Picture HERE COME THE WAVES

Lyric by JOHNNY MERCER
Music by HAROLD ARLEN

Happily

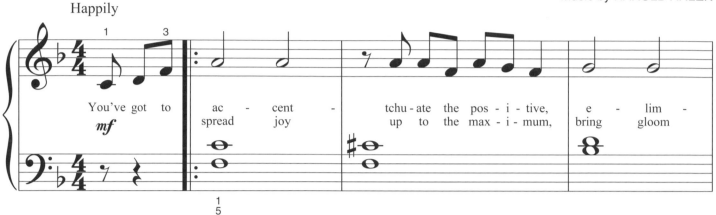

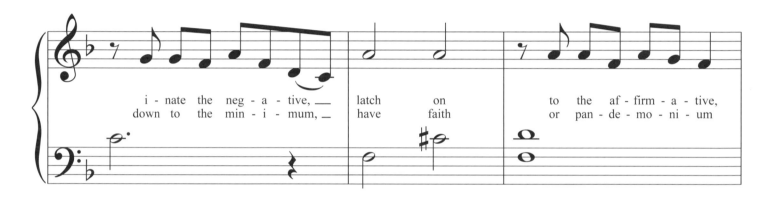

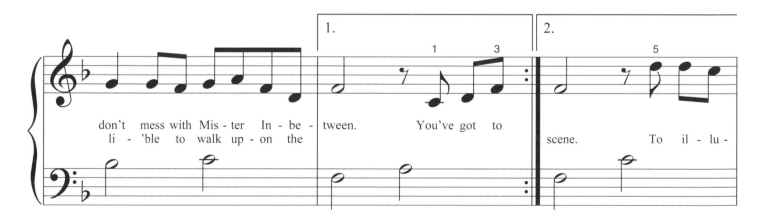

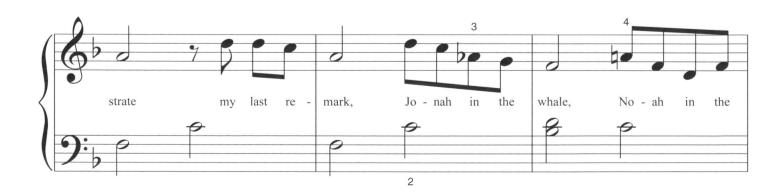

ark.   What did they   do   just when   ev - 'ry - thing looked so   dark?

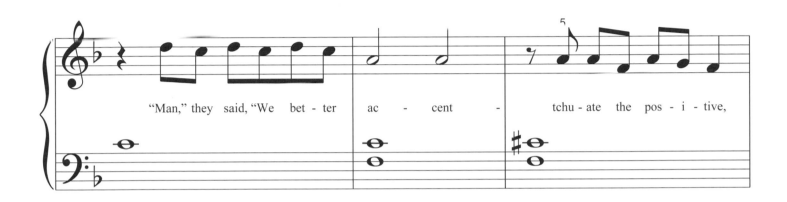

"Man," they said, "We   bet - ter   ac - cent - tchu - ate   the pos - i - tive,

e - lim - i - nate the neg - a - tive, ___   latch   on

to the af - firm - a - tive,   don't mess with Mis - ter In - be - tween."

DON'T WORRY, BE HAPPY

Words and Music by
BOBBY McFERRIN

worry,   be   hap-py.

In ev-'ry life we   have some trou-ble,

2

but when you wor-ry you   make   it   dou-ble. Don't   wor-ry,

be   hap-py.   (Spoken:) Don't   wor-ry, be   hap-py.

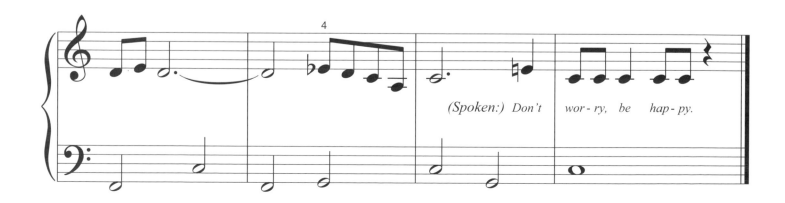

(Spoken:) Don't wor - ry, be hap - py.

HAPPY TOGETHER

Words and Music by GARRY BONNER
and ALAN GORDON

Im - ag - ine me and you, I do.   I think a - bout you
call you up, in - vest a dime, and you say you be -

day and night. It's on - ly right to think a - bout the girl you love and hold her
long to me and ease my mind, im - ag - ine how the world could be so ver - y

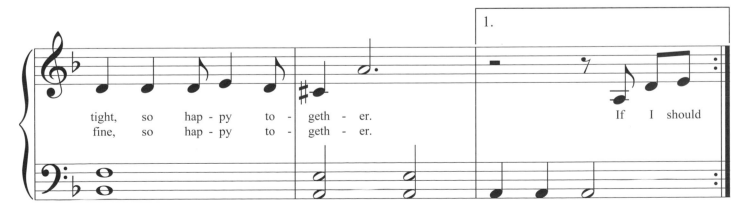

tight, so hap - py to - geth - er.
fine, so hap - py to - geth - er.

1.

If I should

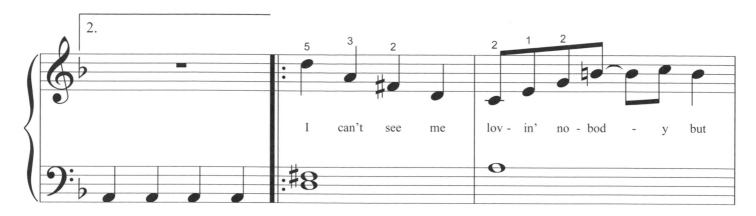

I can't see me lov - in' no - bod - y but

you for all my life. When you're with me,

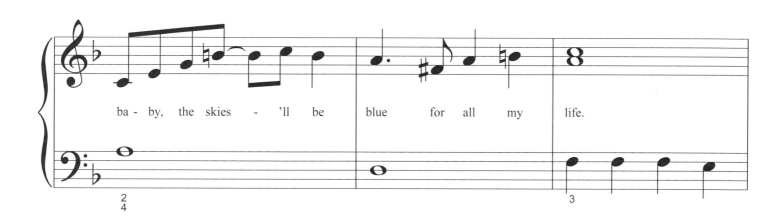

ba - by, the skies - 'll be blue for all my life.

Me and you, and you and me, no mat - ter now they toss the dice, it had to

be. The on - ly one for me is you, and you for me, so hap - py to-

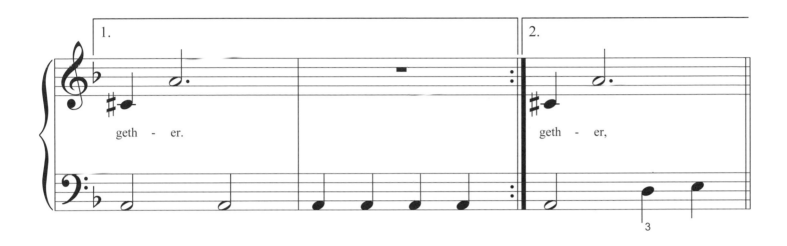

geth - er.

geth - er,

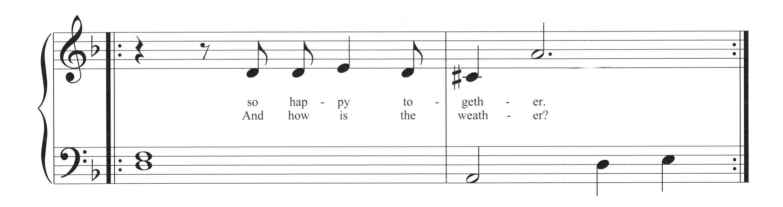

so hap - py to - geth - er.
And how is the weath - er?

So hap - py to - geth - er.

HAPPINESS

from YOU'RE A GOOD MAN, CHARLIE BROWN

Words and Music by
CLARK GESNER

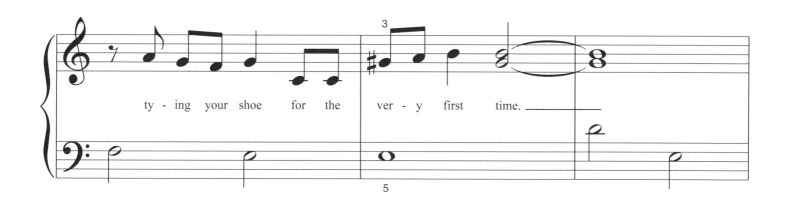

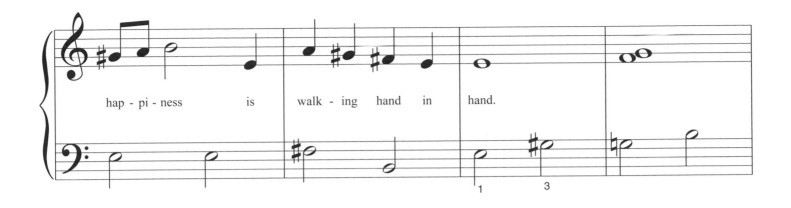

hap - pi - ness   is   walk - ing hand in   hand.

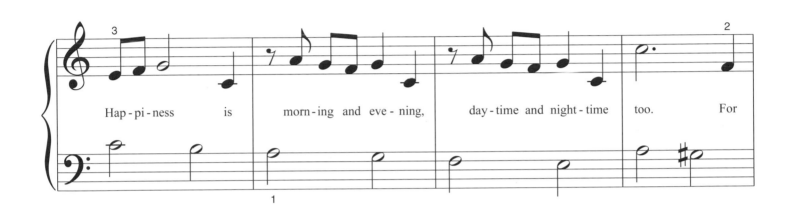

Hap - pi - ness   is   morn - ing and eve - ning,   day - time and night - time   too.   For

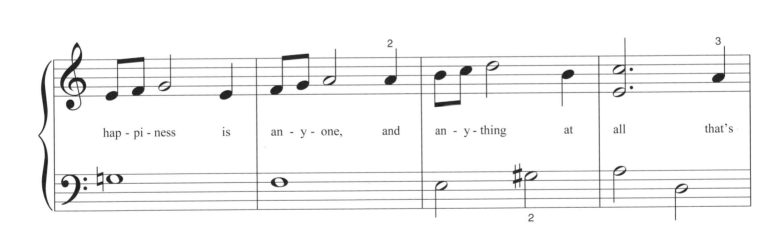

hap - pi - ness   is   an - y - one,   and   an - y - thing   at   all   that's

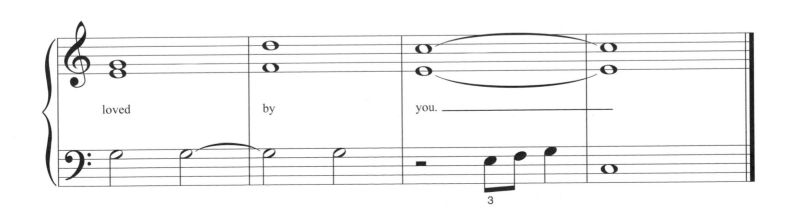

loved   by   you.

HAPPY
from DESPICABLE ME 2

Words and Music by
PHARRELL WILLIAMS

Moderately fast

hot air bal - loon that could go to space

with the air like I don't care, ba - by, by the way.

Huh! Be - cause I'm hap - py.
Clap a - long

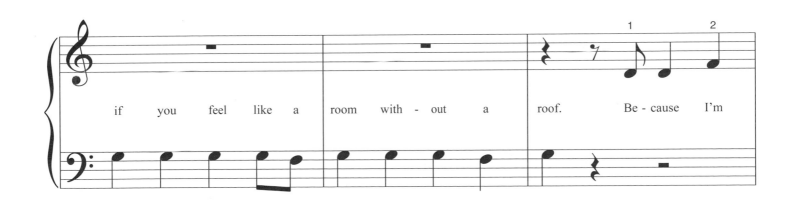

if you feel like a room with - out a roof. Be - cause I'm

hap - py.
Clap a - long   if you feel like   hap - pi - ness is the

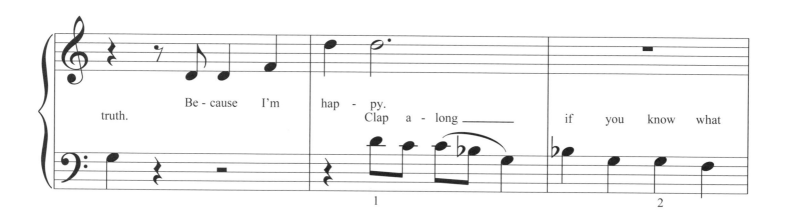

truth.   Be - cause I'm   hap - py.
Clap a - long _____   if you know what

1   2

hap - pi - ness is to   you.   Be - cause I'm   hap - py.
Clap a - long

if you feel like   that's what you wan - na   do.

1

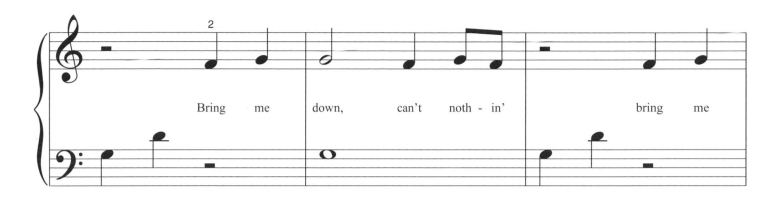

Bring me down, can't noth - in' bring me

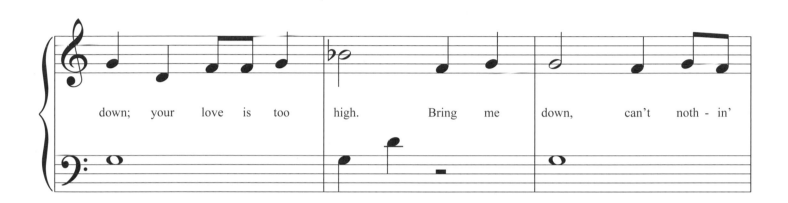

down; your love is too high. Bring me down, can't noth - in'

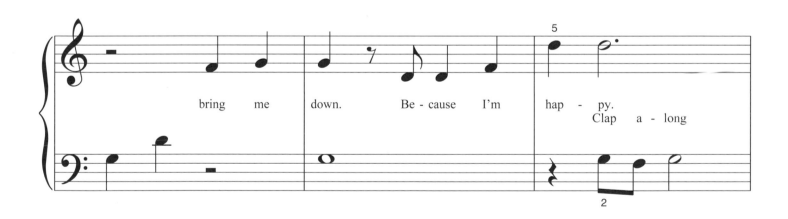

bring me down. Be - cause I'm hap - py.
Clap a - long

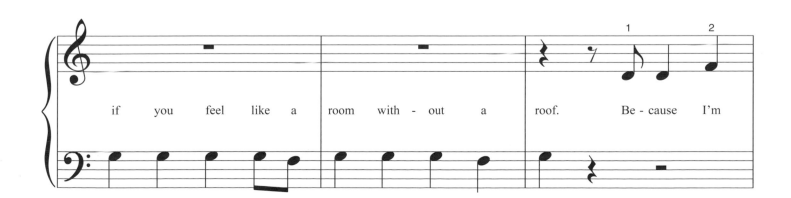

if you feel like a room with - out a roof. Be - cause I'm

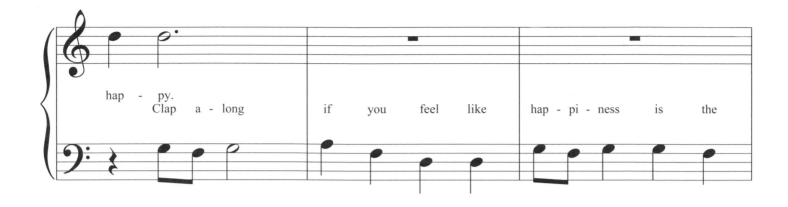

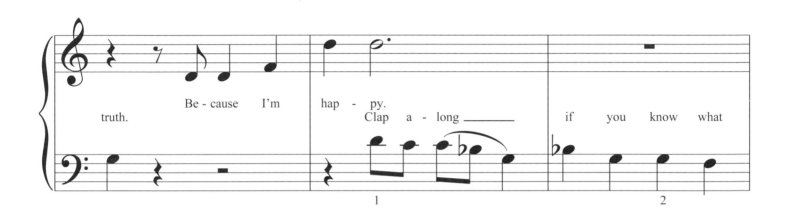

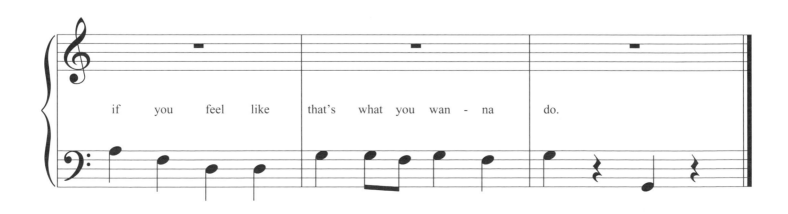

HIGH HOPES
from A HOLE IN THE HEAD

Words by SAMMY CAHN
Music by JAMES VAN HEUSEN

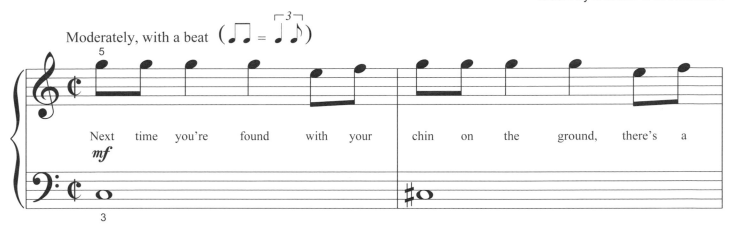

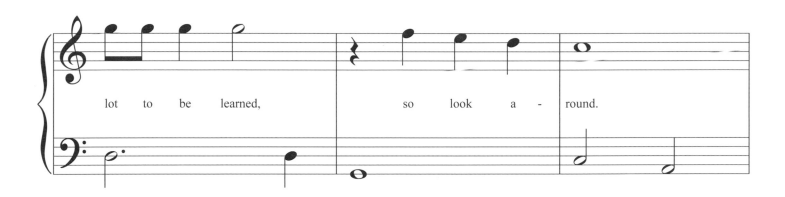

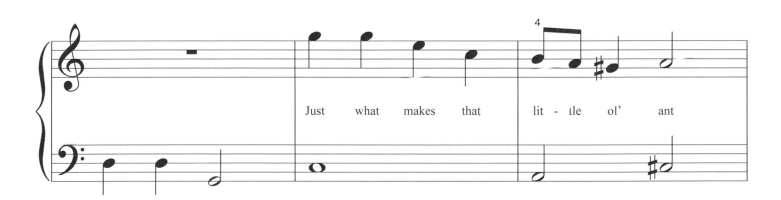

ant can't   move a rub - ber tree   plant. But he's got

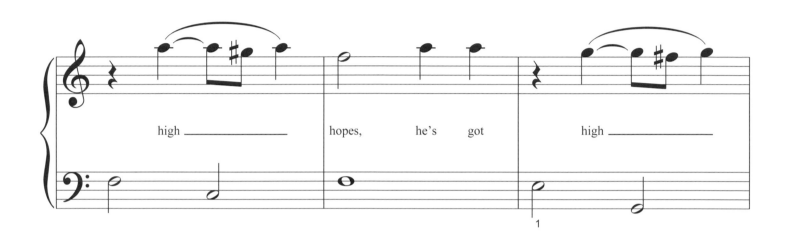

high _____ hopes, he's got   high _____

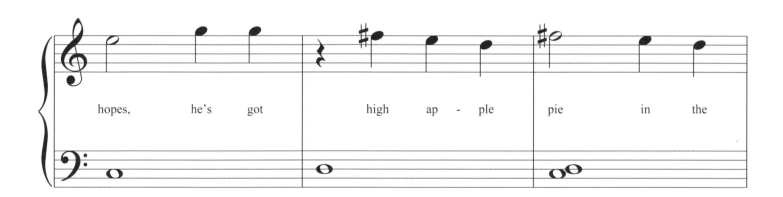

hopes, he's got   high ap - ple   pie in the

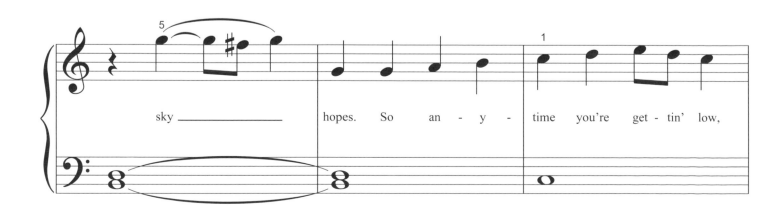

sky _____ hopes. So an - y - time you're get - tin' low,

'stead of let - tin' go, just re - mem - ber that ant.

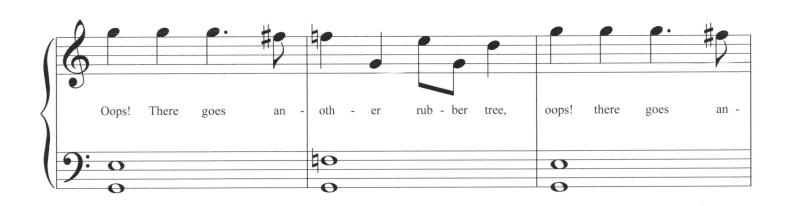

Oops! There goes an - oth - er rub - ber tree, oops! there goes an -

oth - er rub - ber tree, oops! there goes an -

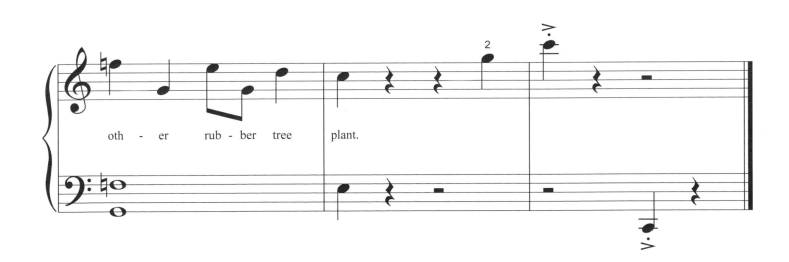

oth - er rub - ber tree plant.

LOVELY DAY

Words and Music by SKIP SCARBOROUGH
and BILL WITHERS

23

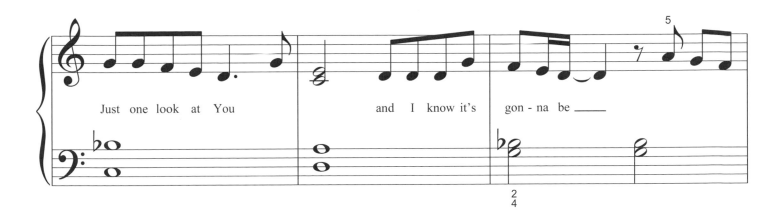

Just one look at You and I know it's gon - na be _____

a love - ly day. Love - ly day, love - ly day,

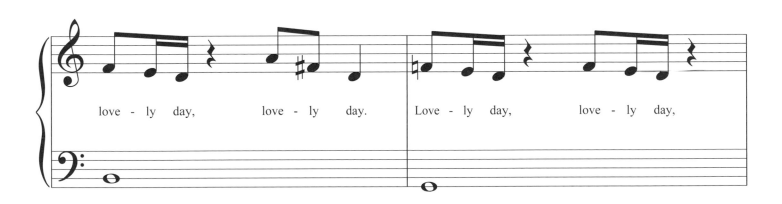

love - ly day, love - ly day. Love - ly day, love - ly day,

love - ly day, love - ly day.

OCTOPUS'S GARDEN

Words and Music by
RICHARD STARKEY

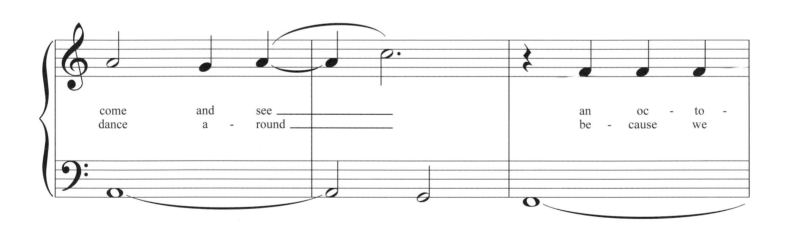

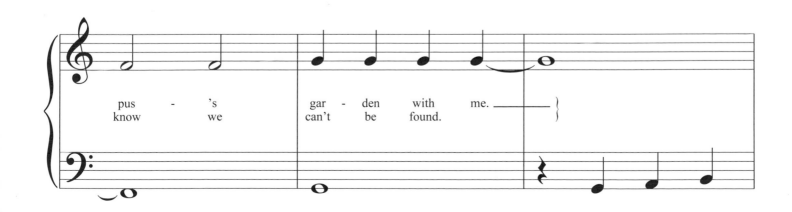

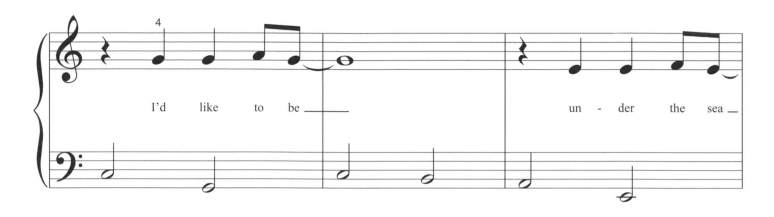

I'd like to be ___ un - der the sea ___

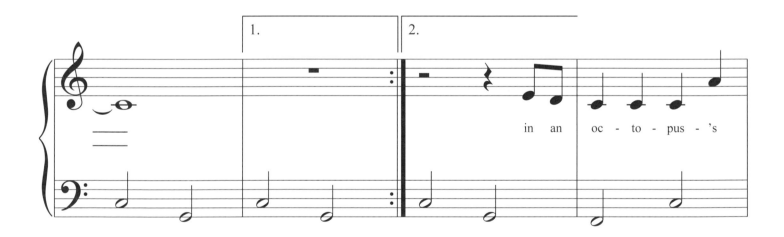

___ in an oc - to - pus - 's gar - den { in the shade. ___
{ with ___ you, ___

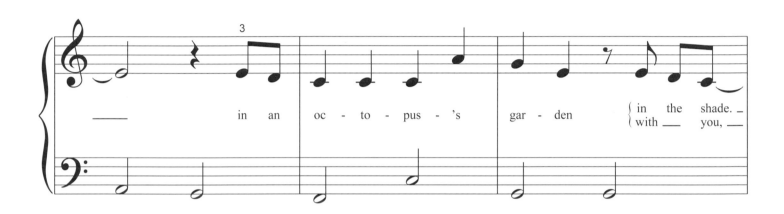

1.

2.

in an oc - to - pus - 's

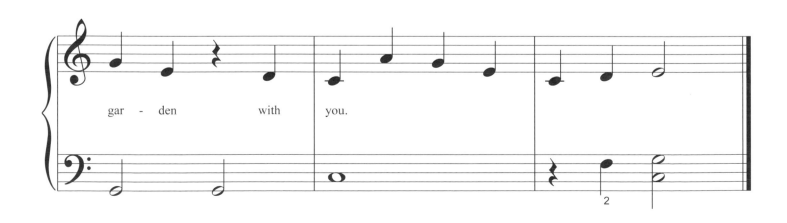

gar - den with you.

SINGIN' IN THE RAIN

from SINGIN' IN THE RAIN

Lyric by ARTHUR FREED
Music by NACIO HERB BROWN

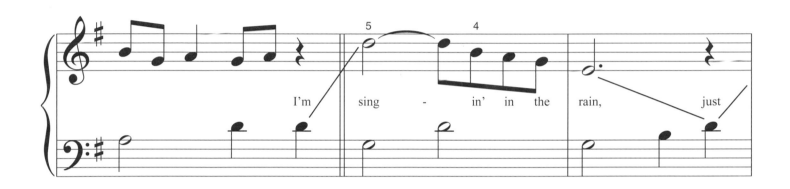

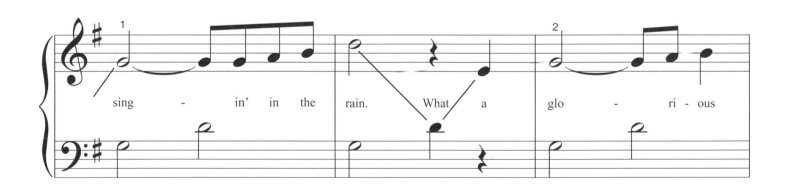

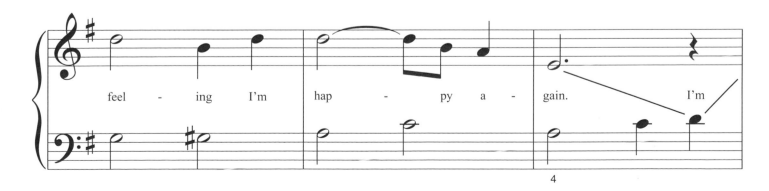

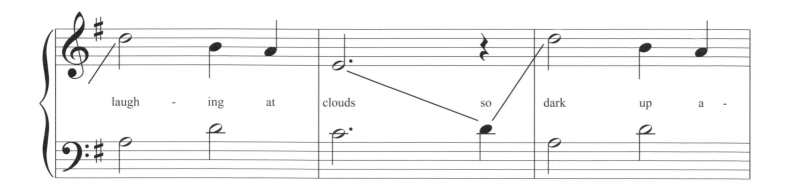

laugh - ing at clouds so dark up a -

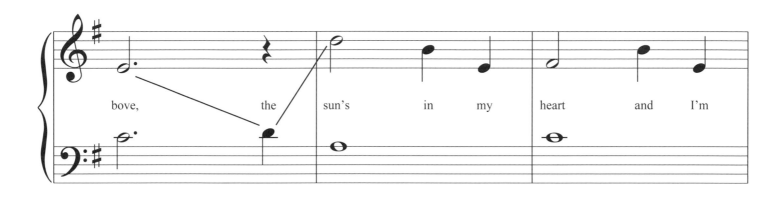

bove, the sun's in my heart and I'm

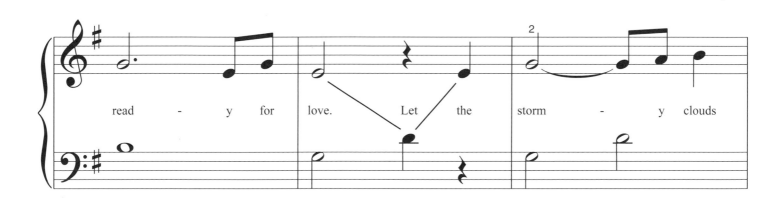

read - y for love. Let the storm - y clouds

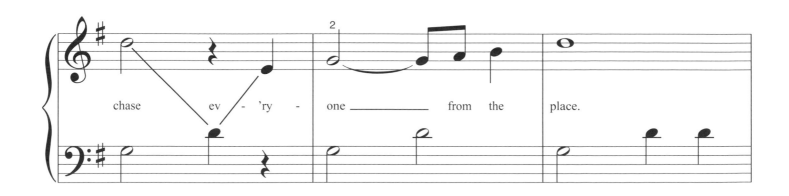

chase ev - 'ry - one _____ from the place.

Come on _____ with the rain, I've a smile on my

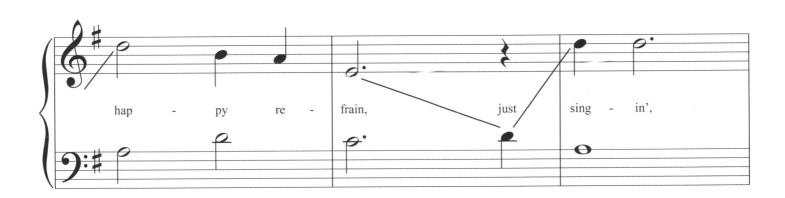

face. I'll walk down the lane with a

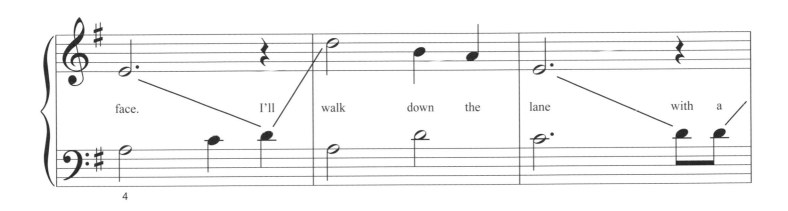

hap - py re - frain, just sing - in',

sing - in' in the rain.

YOU ARE MY SUNSHINE

Words and Music by
JIMMIE DAVIS

The oth-er night, dear, _____ as I lay sleep-ing _____

_____ I dreamed I held you in my arms,

but when I woke, dear, _____ I was mis-tak-en, _____

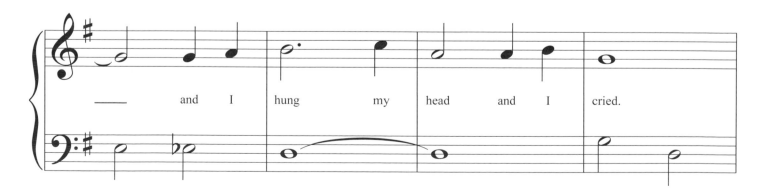

_____ and I hung my head and I cried.

You are my sun - shine, ____ my on - ly sun - shine. ____

____ You make me hap - py ____ when skies are gray.

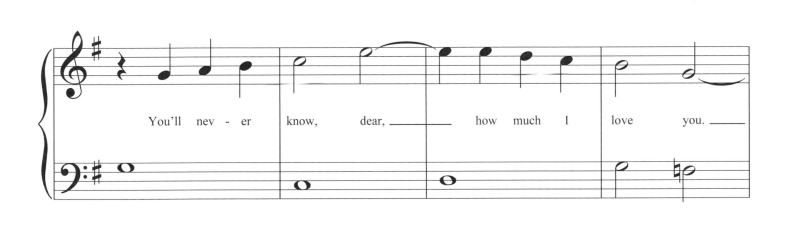

You'll nev - er know, dear, ____ how much I love you. ____

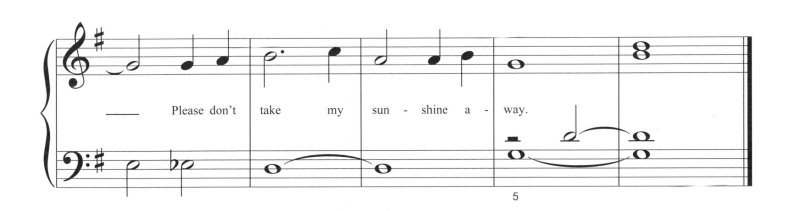

____ Please don't take my sun - shine a - way.

BEGINNING PIANO SOLO

Hal Leonard Beginning Piano Solos are created for students in the first and second years of study. These arrangements include a simple presentation of melody and harmony for a first "solo" experience. See www.halleonard.com for complete song lists.

00153652 The Charlie Brown Collection™ $10.99

00316058 First Book of Disney Solos $12.99

00311065 Jazz Standards $9.95

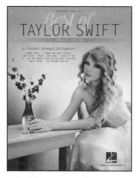

00103239 The Phantom of the Opera $12.99

00175650 Best of Taylor Swift ... $12.99

00156395 Adele $12.99

00311063 Classical Favorites $8.99

00130375 Frozen $12.99

00118420 Best of Carole King ... $10.99

00175142 Pop Hits $10.99

00119401 Tangled $10.99

00306568 The Beatles $12.99

00316082 Contemporary Disney Solos $12.99

00311799 Gospel Hymn Favorites $8.99

00103351 Les Misérables $12.99

00311271 Praise & Worship Favorites $9.95

00110390 10 Fun Favorites $9.99

00307153 Songs of the Beatles $9.99

00311431 Disney Classics $10.99

00311064 Greatest Pop Hits $9.99

00319465 The Lion King $12.99

00316037 The Sound of Music ... $10.99

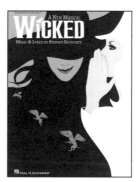

00109365 Wicked $10.99

00279152 Cartoon Favorites $9.99

00264691 Disney Hits $10.99

00319418 It's a Beautiful Day with Mr. Rogers $8.99

00110402 The Most Beautiful Songs Ever $14.99

00110287 Star Wars .. $12.99

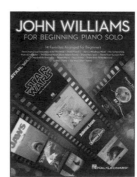

00194545 John Williams $10.99

HAL•LEONARD
www.halleonard.com
Prices, contents and availability are subject to change without notice.
Disney characters and artwork TM & © 2019 Disney